Like a Love Song

Joseph Dziobek
Maia Jansson

Like a Love Song

Copyright © 2025 Joseph Dziobek

Produced and printed by Stillwater River Publications. All rights reserved. Written and produced in the United States of America. This book may not be reproduced or sold in any form without the expressed, written permission of the author(s) and publisher.

Visit our website at
www.StillwaterPress.com
for more information.

First Stillwater River Publications Edition.

ISBN: 978-1-968548-17-9

1 2 3 4 5 6 7 8 9 10

Written by Joseph Dziobek.
Illustrated by Maia Jansson.
Cover & interior book design by Matthew St. Jean.
Published by Stillwater River Publications,
West Warwick, RI, USA.

The views and opinions expressed in this book are solely those of the author(s) and do not necessarily reflect the views and opinions of the publisher.

To my wife, Linda, for her love and inspiration and to Maia Jansson for her extraordinary illustrations that bring my verse to life. Special thanks to Dr. John Winkelman without whom this book would not have been completed.

—Joseph

To my parents for their love and teachings. To my friends for always supporting my dreams. Special thanks to Joe Dziobek for entrusting me with this project and for the guidance along the way.

—Maia

From Us

Like a Love Song sums up my feelings about living in South County. The joy of seeing deer in my meadow, fishermen going through the channel as the sun rises over Galilee, discovering a piece of sea glass that came in with the tide—I love this place, its people, and the feelings that it stirs up inside of me. This is what I write about, my community, my home.

—Joseph

Creating art is akin to breathing. The artwork I create derives from many sources—pre-existing text, dreams, memories, and nature are my biggest influences. I approach art the same way I approached playing as a child—exploratory and whimsical.

The poems Joe wrote resonated with my experience growing up in Narragansett—from sunburnt beach trips with my family to sea-scented walks through the woods. You can find a part of me in the illustrations throughout this book.

—Maia

Butterflies and Rainbows

Butterflies and rainbows
Here but a moment, then gone
But in that moment of surprise
They make our world brighter
Like a love song

Friend

Digging in the ground
Is popular with those around
Such as toads and snakes
And robins I have found
One robin in particular
I named him Friend
Came by to check me out one day
And has been coming ever since

The Bond

When I wake in the morning
I go to the window to see
If my white tailed friends
Are there to greet me
I look toward the meadow
And then toward the pond
Though we've never formally met
I feel the bond

Waves

Waves like my emotions
Greet me at the shore
What am I to make of them
They're here and then they're gone
Beyond where my eyes can see
To disappear once more
Until the day that I return
To embrace them as before

My Maker

The stillness of the morning
Lies in wait for me
As I walk down to the harbor
The closer I will be
To My Maker and that feeling
As I witness the dawn of light
The essence of my being
Sprung from the darkness of night

Peace of Mind

Salt air in my hair
Morning mist in my eyes
It's along these calming waters
I find peace of mind
From the worries that follow me
Like a shadow of my making
It's here I lay them down
With every step I'm taking

Sea Glass

What is it about sea glass
That captivates me so
Is it the color or the smoothness
Or the history I want to know
How did it come about
Who held it before me
Did it come from far away
Or been buried beneath my feet

Reluctantly

Reluctantly, I leave the shore
The water's ebb and flow
White foam on the deserted beach
But I am not alone
I feel a presence surrounding me
I am at peace
I walk away looking back
At my childhood memories

The Shoreline

The shoreline lies littered
With once living things
Washed up by the tide
To live with uncertainty
Will the tide take the remains
Back into the sea
Or will someone else come along
And pocket two or three

Solitude

Morning light on the marsh
Beckons me to stay
But what of my responsibilities
Can I just put them away
I think not
They're forever on my mind
But drinking in this moment now
Is the best use of my time

Resilience

The stately old mansion
Facing wind and waves
Proudly holding on
Trying to save face
It's moss-covered roof
And weathered clapboard skin
Has stood the test of time
And will do so again

The Sounds of Spring

The sounds of spring
Like a chorus at Christmas
Welcoming in the season
Need there be anything more
Than a walk to the shore
To convince me
Of life beyond reason

Buoy #2

It sits floating in the channel
It's job never done
It's there to guide the boats
That pass by it one by one
Most people don't appreciate
The job that it does
Some might say that's true
For all of us

Block Island

I come here in the early morning
To see if I can see
The island in the distance
That is calling out to me
Sometimes the fog
Shields her from my eyes
But this day I see her clearly
Just standing by

Bicycles
So much more
Than two wheels and a frame
This foot pedal wonder
That's taken me to countless places I can't name
But it's the morning rides that mean the most
With my two neighbors and dear friends
With every mile that we ride
I feel our friendship deepen

East Matunuck in Winter

No crowds, no cars in line
To be the first to bask in the sunshine
Just an occasional passerby
Alone in thought
On my morning walk, am I

Surfers

I view them from the road
Waiting for the perfect wave
Out beyond the white water
Bobbing in wetsuits so brave
Patience, it takes patience
To catch the perfect wave
But when they do I too
Am rooting they take it all the way

Salt Pond

I walk along the wooded trails
With anticipation
Of the beauty and tranquility
That awaits at my destination
At last, I reach the salt pond
That Mother Nature did create
I thank her for her generosity
This gift of great escape

Paradise

The salty air
The offshore wind
If I were to build a paradise
This is where I would begin
The endless stretch of beaches
To watch the sun rise and fall
The changing of the seasons
Yes, I feel I have it all

Butterflies and Rainbows
MELODY AND LYRICS BY JOSEPH DZIOBEK

Butterflies and rainbows
Here but a moment then gone
But in that moment of surprise
Make our world brighter
Like a love song
Love is a wonderful feeling
When all the world seems right
I can't wait for the end of the day
To go together thru life

Can you see the beauty around us
Hear the music in your heart
Feel the love I've been feeling for you
Right from the start
Take me in your arms
Tell me you love me too
Cause my love like a beautiful love song
Never stops playing for you

I've never felt this way before
Never knew what love could do
I can move mountains
Turn your grey skies to blue
We've got a lifetime of living
Left for us to do
And there's no one else I'd rather
Do it with than you

Can you see the beauty around us
Hear the music in your heart
Feel the love I've been feeling for you
Right from the start
Take me in your arms
Tell me you love me too
Cause my love like a beautiful love song
Never stops playing for you

Oh it's true
Butterflies and rainbows
I see them everywhere I'm with you

Can you see the beauty around us
Hear the music in your heart
Feel the love I've been feeling for you
Right from the start
Take me in your arms
Tell me you love me too
Cause my love like a beautiful love song
Never stops playing for you
With butterflies and rainbows too

SCAN TO LISTEN

Joseph Dziobek found his calling after visiting a relative in a psychiatric hospital. Struck by the stark nature of the facility and hopelessness that pervaded the room, he dedicated his life to creating alternatives in the community with a strong emphasis on the arts. In 2013, he received the Impact Award for Visionary Leadership from the National Council for Community Behavioral Healthcare.

A prolific singer/songwriter and poet, he teamed up with legendary artists to record a number of songs, among them the "Caregiver's Song" (2010), "Season of Light" (2013), and "Bend But Not Break" (2014), written for and recorded by a formerly homeless mental health consumer. "Butterflies and Rainbows," a song he wrote, recorded, and produced, was released in May 2025. He also wrote a one-act play titled "The Faces of Homelessness," which was performed by the Contemporary Theater Company in 2017. *Like a Love Song* is his first published book of poems. He resides with his wife, Linda, in Snug Harbor, Rhode Island.

Maia Jansson is an illustrator and designer currently based in Rhode Island. She attended the Savannah College of Art and Design, where she received a BFA in Illustration for Publication. In her free time, she enjoys reading, writing, and listening to music. You can find her at www.maiajansson.com.

www.ingramcontent.com/pod-product-compliance
Lightning Source LLC
Chambersburg PA
CBRC091204010526
44107CB00021B/1241